Poetry
Animal Homes

my home in the water

By J. Patrick Lewis

Children's Press®
An Imprint of Scholastic Inc.

Library of Congress Cataloging-in-Publication Data
Names: Lewis, J. Patrick, author.
Title: My home in the water/by J. Patrick Lewis.
Description: New York, NY: Children's Press, An Imprint of Scholastic Inc., 2017.
| Series: Rookie poetry. Animal homes | Includes index.
Identifiers: LCCN 2016030838| ISBN 9780531228746 (library binding)
| ISBN 9780531230091 (pbk.)
Subjects: LCSH: Aquatic animals—Juvenile literature.
Classification: LCC QL122.2 .L49 2017 | DDC 591.76—dc23
LC record available at https://lccn.loc.gov/2016030838

Produced by Spooky Cheetah Press
Design by Anna Tunick

Printed in China 62

1 2 3 4 5 6 7 8 9 10 R 26 25 24 23 22 21 20 19 18 17

Photos ©: cover: Klein and Hubert/Minden Pictures; back cover background: Kryssia Campos/Getty Images; back cover gorilla: John
Lund/Getty Images; back cover boa constrictor: Pete Oxford/Minden Pictures; back cover toucan: Caroline von Tuempling/Getty Images;
cloud vector throughout: Freepik.com; leaf vector throughout: gomarce/Vecteezy; 1: ronnybas/Shutterstock, Inc.; 2-3: Martin Harvey/Getty
Images; 5: Matthew Williams-Ellis/Getty Images; 7: John Lund/Getty Images; 9: W. Perry Conway/Getty Images; 11: Pete Oxford/Minden Pictures;
13: Anup Shah/Minden Pictures; 15: Caroline von Tuempling/Getty Images; 17: Mchugh Tom/Getty Images; 19 background: MoreISO/Getty Images; 19
gorilla: John Lund/Getty Images; 19 jaguar: W. Perry Conway/Getty Images; 19 boa constrictor: Pete Oxford/Minden Pictures; 19 monkey: Anup Shah/
Minden Pictures; 19 toucan: Caroline von Tuempling/Getty Images; 19 centipede: Mchugh Tom/Getty Images; 20 left: ilovezion/Shutterstock, Inc.; 20
center right: Luiz Claudio Marigo/Minden Pictures; 20 center left: John Lund/Getty Images; 20 right: Pete Oxford/Minden Pictures; 21 left: The Africa
Image Library/Alamy Images; 21 center left: Madlen/Shutterstock, Inc.; 21 center right: rodho/iStockphoto; 21 right: Mchugh Tom/Getty Images; 21
center: Caroline von Tuempling/Getty Images; 23 center top: Elena Kalistratova/Getty Images; 23 top: Caroline von Tuempling/Getty Images; 23 center:
Mchugh Tom/Getty Images; 23 center bottom: Pete Oxford/Minden Pictures; 23 bottom: W. Perry Conway/Getty Images.

table of contents

welcome to the water

It covers two-thirds of the planet.
Is it blue? Is it green? In between?
It is home to strange creatures,
  gigantic and tiny,
some widely known, some yet unseen.

The aquatic **biome** includes all the habitats that are made up mostly of water. It is the biggest biome on the planet.

blue whale

Happy, she sings a day-long song
that travels for miles, seeming never to stop.
When not making waves and racing big ships,
just for fun she blows her top.

Blue whales are the largest animals that have ever lived on Earth.

octopus

To an octopus luncheon for nine,
these comrades-in-arms come to dine.
But when hugging each other
  —what **suckers**, oh brother!—
they look like a great ball of twine.

An octopus can change its color to brown, gray, green, blue, or even pink to match its surroundings!

alligator & crocodile

Al's and Croc's enormous **snouts**
are odd, and here's the key:
Al's looks a lot like the letter U;
Croc's looks like the letter V.

Alligators can be found in North America and China. Crocodiles live everywhere but Antarctica and Europe.

minnow

Never go **wading** with minnows.
A minnow, as everyone knows,
is an inch of a fellow, who tickles you
  —Hello!—
and nibbles the tops of your toes!

Minnows travel in large schools. This keeps them safe from predators.

shark

It's amazing to think that there are
over 500 **species** of shark,
and each one is scarier than
the next one out there in the dark!

Sharks lose their teeth a lot and have to grow new ones. This hammerhead shark loses about 35,000 in its lifetime!

green sea turtle

I am a helmet in the sea,
but so afraid of strangers,
I am extremely shy because
the ocean's full of dangers.

The green sea turtle is one of the largest turtles on Earth.

humid homes

A lake is a trout's recreation;
a river's a minnow's whirlpool;
the ocean is one destination
where just about everything's cool.

The animals shown in this book are on these pages. Can you find them all?

fact files

	Blue Whale	Octopus	Alligator & Crocodile
HOW BIG AM I?	up to 100 feet long (*about the length of a basketball court*)	up to 3 feet long (*as long as a yardstick*)	up to 15 feet long (**A**) up to 23 feet long (**C**) (*longer than a car*)
HOW MUCH DO I WEIGH?	up to 200 tons (*more than 2,000 adults*)	up to 22 pounds (*about the same as a car tire*)	up to 1,000 (**A**) or 2,000 (**C**) pounds (*as much as two or four motorcycles*)
WHAT DO I EAT?	krill	crabs, mollusks, crayfish	fish, snakes, turtles, small mammals (**A**) fish, birds, crabs, frogs (**C**)

Minnow	Hammerhead Shark	Green Sea Turtle
less than 4 inches long *(about as long as a credit card)*	up to 20 feet long *(as long as a giraffe is tall)*	up to 5 feet long *(almost as long as a bicycle)*
.5 ounces *(about half as much as a penny)*	up to 1,000 pounds *(as much as five gorillas)*	up to 700 pounds *(more than a vending machine)*
plants, insects	stingrays, crabs, squid	sea grasses, jellyfish, crabs

water...the wet facts

1. **The water ecosystem is made up of both freshwater and salt water.** Freshwater includes rivers, lakes, and ponds. Salt water is found in oceans and seas.

2. **Water is the largest biome on the planet.** It takes up more than 70% of Earth's surface.

3. **Scientists think that up to 80% of all life on Earth can be found in the oceans.** Zooplankton, some of the tiniest animals on the planet, live there. The ocean is also home to the largest animal on Earth—the blue whale.

4. **About 90% of all the volcanic activity on Earth takes place in the ocean.** The ocean is also home to Earth's largest mountain range.

5. **Without water, life on Earth would not be possible.** Our bodies need water to function. Water also enables us to grow the food we need to eat.

glossary

biome (BYE-ohm): Regions in the world with similar weather, temperature, animals, and plants.

snouts (SNOWTS): The front part of an animal's head, including nose, mouth, and jaws.

species (SPEE-sheez): Groups of animals or plants that are similar and can produce young animals or plants.

suckers (SUHK-urz): A body part of certain animals that is used to stick to surfaces.

wading (WAYD-ing): Walking through water.

index

facts for now

Visit this Scholastic Web site to learn more about water habitats and download the Teaching Guide for this series: **www.factsfornow.scholastic.com**
Enter the keyword **Water**

about the author

J. Patrick Lewis has published 100 children's picture and poetry books to date, with a wide variety of publishers. The Poetry Foundation named him the third U.S. Children's Poet Laureate.